Life's Curve Balls: Storms that Change Us

Courtney Fraser

Life's Curve Balls: Storms that Change Us ©
2023 Courtney Fraser

All rights reserved.

Courtney Fraser asserts the moral right to be identified as the author of this work.

Presentation by *BookLeaf Publishing*

Web: www.bookleafpub.com

E-mail: info@bookleafpub.com

ISBN: 9789358366259

First edition 2023

ACKNOWLEDGEMENT

God: Thank first and foremost to God. I would not have gotten through writing these poems without the strength and wisdom you provided me with every day I was writing a poem for this book. Throughout my life, you have protected me, given me strength, and given me wisdom when I needed it the most.

Dr. Sabrina Rojek: Thank you for everything you have done to help me discover both my written and spoken voices matter. I would not have even thought of taking on a challenge, such as writing 21 poems in 21 days about life's curveballs when we started working together back in late 2020.

Danielle Pomerleau: Thank you for helping me realize how I was overthinking this section and the preface section of this book. Once you told me that there was no need to stress and lay it on the Lord, I stopped and thought more about it. It also reminded me that writing these sections just means that the book is close to being complete.

Nick and Megan Unsworth: Thank you for the community you have built during the pandemic.

Thank you also for your constant commitment to the Life on Fire family. Without the two of you, I would not have had a total of 5 books written and published over these last 3+ years.

Kyla Pollard: Thank you for encouraging me after I wrote the "dissociation" and "depression" poems. From your encouragement, I realized how important it was to include them in this book. Thank you for your friendship and for helping me through some tough life curveballs and some of my toughest life storms.

Scott Dillon: Thank you for helping me through some difficult times that life has thrown at me recently. It added to the strength I got from God to continue writing these poems. I kept remembering what you taught me in our sessions together as I was writing this book.

Learning Disability

Lower expectations
Embarrassment happens because of the
treatment received
Accommodations
Resource
Nervous about being bullied
Individualized Education Plan
Never feel safe because of questions asked by
peers
Goals need to be met every year

Daily challenges
Identity based on a label
Special Education
Abused emotionally and verbally by society
Bury true selves and emotions
Injured by the words others use towards them or
about them
Looked down upon
Innocence was taken away
They might need therapies
Youthful thinking

TBI

Troublesome
Rough
Annoying
Unfortunate
Memory problems
Adjustments needed
Terrible
Identity crisis
Calendar needed to keep things straight

Baseline tests done
Relearn
Accepting is difficult
Impacts life going forward
New normal

Interests might change
Needs change
Journey
Undergo surgery
Rehab
Yesterday was different

PTSD

Physical reactions
Overstimulation
Safety questioned
Triggered

Therapy might be needed
Rational thought goes out the window
Acceptance of diagnosis is difficult
Unique causes
Military members are not the only ones that get
it
Aggravation that it doesn't seem to go away
Thoughts of past events
Increase in reliance on others
Challenging

Sense of self changes
Troublesome reactions
Return to normalcy after a trigger takes a while
Elsewhere in time
Scars can be unseen by others
Sensitive to loud noises

Disorienting experience
Internal pain shows outwardly

Shame regarding not being over the trauma
Overpowering flashbacks
Replay of trauma through nightmares
Disheartening whenever it returns with a
vengeance
Emergency signal in the brain goes off
Returning to reality is difficult and takes time

PTE

PTE
Personality changes
Ongoing checkups
Seizures
Triggers

Tense muscles
Responding to things being said to you is
difficult
Acceptance of diagnosis is difficult
Urgent help is needed if the seizure goes longer
than 5 minutes
Management through medications
Afraid of the next seizure
Thoughts of suicide
Impatient while figuring out treatment
Changes to life need to be made

Electrical misfiring in the brain
Photosensitive
Impossible to ignore
Landmine of challenges
Embarrassment ensues after the seizure
Prescriptions
Stigma
Yesterday always feels the same as today

Depression

Dissociate
Energy is lacking
Passions go out the door
Relief seems far away
Emotions are all over the place
Suicidal thoughts
Self-harm is hard not to think about
Irrational thoughts
Optimism is a no go
Narrow tunnel of vision

Suicide

Self-harm feels like the only solution to
Unbelievable unseen pain
Individual reasons
Clear thinking goes out the window
Instant questioning by those left behind
Devastating
Emotional

Dissociation

Delirious daze
Identity crisis
Scary
Separation from reality
Out of sorts
Cold
Internal survival system
Anger
Terrible
Induced by trauma
On a different planet
Normalcy is gone

Anxiety

Alarm on high alert
Nervous energy
Xanax is a medication that might be prescribed
Interrupts life as you know it
Extreme fear
Thief of joy and rest
Yearn for calm

ADHD

All over the place
Therapy might be needed
Time thief
Emotional overwhelm
Neurodiverse
Thinking is difficult
Impulsive
Optimism is hard
Nurse practitioners help treat

Diagnosis might take a while
Evaluation by a doctor is needed
Focus issues
Intense thoughts and feelings
Capacity of energy levels is low
Individual experiences
Transitions are hard

Hard time with memory
Youthful thinking
Possible comorbidity with epilepsy
Education can be difficult
Rapid changes in what they are doing
Anxiety
Concentration is difficult

Trapped feeling
Identity challenges
Value similar things that others do
Impatience is a problem
Troublesome thoughts
Yawning a lot despite not being tired

Decisiveness is difficult
Independence might look different
Sense of satisfaction is low
Overbook themselves
Restless
Differences in how we think
Excitement rollercoaster
Relief wanted

Thyroid

Trouble
Hyperthyroid
Yesterday was different
Results from bloodwork done are not fun
Overactive
Increase in thyroid hormone production
Depression

Trauma

Changes you as a person
You no longer feel invincible
Negative thoughts and feelings worsen
At first, the long-term effects are inconceivable

Each trauma causes issues with memory
You lose huge chunks of time from your life
It hurts both physically and mentally
It causes strife

Bullying

They say words don't hurt
That is not true though
Numb the pain with dessert
Self-confidence and self-esteem are low

Hurt people hurt people is a phrase that is said
That does not help the pain
Negative thoughts go through your head
It feels as if your emotions remain

PCOS

You get diagnosed with Polycystic Ovary
Syndrome
It causes irregular periods
Something felt off and now the answer to what
hits home
It deals with your interiors

Might have spottiness
Have to do biopsies
Pain from it can cause grogginess
However, you can still do your hobbies

Unemployment

Apply for benefits
Just to find out you don't qualify
Some people are still instrumentalists
No need to apologize

More like underemployment payments
Feel that you are not worthy
We consider those that apply to be claimants
It is definitely a journey

Alzheimer's and Dementia

Slow decline
Not the same person you knew
Relationships are redefined
Hard to see it from their point of view

Memory issues
Sad to watch them change
You might need many tissues
It feels strange

Gun In School

It was just a normal school day
Nothing seemed off
All of sudden everything was in disarray
I wanted things to go back to how they were
before

They brought in no outside counselor
There was no school shooting
My school did not have a chancellor
Sadness caused eye drooping

Military Service

Go through a lot of training
Leave behind family and friends
There is nothing about it that is entertaining
Your tribe of people expands

Mental Health can be a problem once you return
You are no longer the same person you were
before you joined
What is reality and what is not reality is hard to
discern
There are situations you might avoid

Surprise Uncle

You are told you have another uncle
Your response is you're kidding me
Believing the news is a struggle
Yet at the same time, it feels like a jubilee

You find out in the middle of a global pandemic
It takes until seeing your obituary to find out the
uncle's name
How you react when you first meet him is not
academic
You are no longer the same

Hospitalizations

Taken for different reasons
One is medical
Go during different seasons
Patients are skeptical

Another reason is mental health
Either way, you can possibly get Post Traumatic
Stress Disorder
Admitting you need help for your mental health
shows strength
Going between mental health and the medical
unit you need a transporter

Medications

Feel like a guinea pig
A struggle to find the correct medication
The deal is pretty big
Might need a medication combination

Side effects are horrible
Questions arise
Medications might be unaffordable
There are many things to consider and analyze

COVID-19

Global pandemic
A new way of life
Research is academic
Causes strife

Vaccine created
You get flack for decisions made
Feel like your value as a person is degraded
Work from home to get paid

New technology discovered
Easier to take more breaks
Some people never recovered
There are high stakes

Might need a doctor's exemption
Changes perception